NORMAL WOMEN in SPORT

Contents

Written by Philippa Gregory

Illustrated by Monica Auriemma

Collins

1 Princesses in Towers or Sporty Women?

I bet you think of women in the "olden days" as princesses in a tower, rather than super-strong sportswomen?

Think again! We're going to show you the truth about the history of women in sport.

Meet Agnes Hotot. She lived way back in the 1300s. Her father had an argument with his enemy, and they agreed to fight it out as knights, **jousting** on horseback.

Agnes's father fell ill and Agnes, who was only a teenager, secretly took his place. She put on his heavy armour, grabbed his **lance**, thundered down the track on his enormous warhorse, and knocked the other jouster off his horse. Everyone cheered when she took off her helmet and revealed that she was a girl!

Brave Agnes Hotot was not alone. Hundreds of women in medieval England were jousters, archers and hunters. Some of them went up against men in teams! Other women were famous runners and fighters. We know very little about all of them – they have vanished from history.

Weak and foolish

The first ever books were written by men in the 700s. These men were taught by the Church that women were weak and foolish. Eight hundred years later, women started to write more truthfully about themselves, but it was too late to set the record straight and – worse! – many women believed what the old books said about them.

Be ladylike!

By the 1800s, schools, families and even doctors taught that girls should be quiet and ladylike. Their long skirts meant they could not run; their tight corsets meant they could not breathe or eat well. It was impossible for them to play sports, and in the 1900s, women were told that sport would make them ill. Doctors said that running long distances would make women runners grow hair on their backs!

DO TRY THIS AT HOME! – you can run really fast and you won't grow hair on your back!

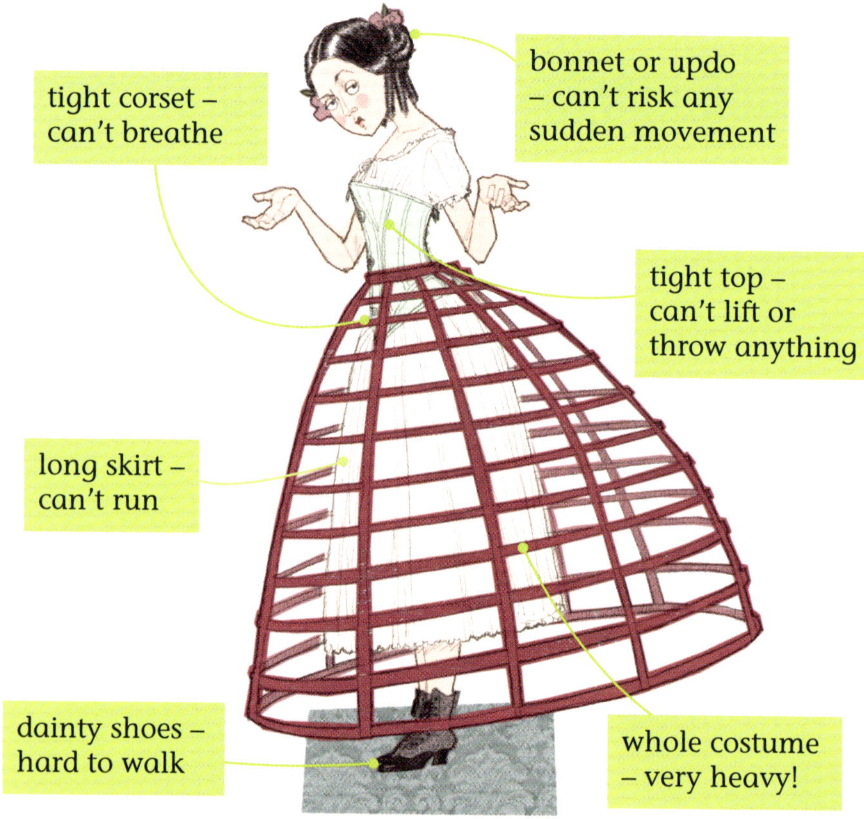

This story begins almost one thousand years ago. All kinds of women have played games and sports throughout history – even when no one was watching or cheering them on.

This book is about all these women.

2 Castles and Kings

... and queens and working women!

1066–1642

William the Conqueror invades England.

The Black Death kills so many workers that women get equal pay.

Elizabeth I is queen – but women are paid less and must stay at home by law!

1066

1348–1349

1558–1603

When William the Conqueror and the Norman army invaded England in 1066, they brought in strict rules against women. Women couldn't own a home, leave a bad husband or run a business. Women worked long hours in the fields and towns, gave birth and fed and clothed the family.

Witch-hunts accuse women, especially poor women, of being witches.

1600s

English **Civil War** starts. Women in the armies are called "she-soldiers".

1642

Fire walkers

We can see women acrobats, dancers, jugglers and **fire walkers** in old drawings. Troops of women went from town to town putting on shows in castles and marketplaces.

We know the stage name of one woman acrobat who performed at the Christmas feast for King Edward I in 1296. She called herself Matilda Makejoy.

Stoolball

Women who milked cows on farms – known as milkmaids – invented their own game called “stoolball”. They used their three-legged stool as a wicket, or as a base, like in rounders. Stoolball is still played today.

Playing at ball

"Playing at ball" was olden days football! Teams kicked, threw and tackled a ball, or even a bundle of rags, between villages until one village won it. It was a rough game with no rules, and everyone could play. We only know about it because the lords of the villages kept banning it. But girls and boys kept playing!

A poem from the 1500s describes how girls tucked up their long dresses so that they could play the game.

"... with skirts tucked very high,
with girls at football played."

Women were known as fast runners and strong fighters. Games like playing at ball need speed and strength.

Hunters and fisherwomen

Rich women hunted on horses with bows and arrows. They were also famous for training falcons. One writer, John of Salisbury, admitted that ladies were better falconers than men!

The first person to ever write about fly fishing in England was a nun: Juliana Berners, born in 1388. She had learned to write at her **convent**.

Juliana Berners

3 Women Fight Back

In 1649, the people won the Civil War against King Charles I, beheaded the king and elected a **parliament** instead.

1640-1800

1642–1649

English Civil War. The people fight against the king and behead him.

1649–1660

A new parliament rules England without a king or queen and bans sport!

1660–1685

Charles II comes back as king of England and allows sports again.

The new parliament was very strict and banned almost all sports and entertainment.

Prince Charles, the king's son, came back to England in 1660 and was crowned king. He loved sports, so sportswomen had the chance to play again.

1700s

Rich landlords put KEEP OUT signs on village lands. Poor women fight back.

1750s

Food prices rise – poor women try to set fair prices.

1790s

Fewer jobs on the land force poor women into towns.

Running

Huge running races were open to men and women with big prize money for the fastest runners. Women mostly ran barefoot, often over greater distances than the men.

Women often ran in their **petticoats** so their long dresses didn't get in the way. In Manchester, in 1681, women raced each other for the prize of a petticoat. Another race was run down Pall Mall, London, in 1732 with lords and ladies watching from the windows and balconies of their grand houses.

Football

The first ever proper football match was played by women in 1726! Six women were on each side of a grass pitch that was usually used for bowling. They met in the town of Bath for a "friendly" match on weekdays, and on Sundays people paid to watch the women play.

Cricket

Cricket was popular from 1660, but "the greatest cricket match" ever played was in 1745, in Reading, between two women's teams: the Bramley Maids in blue ribbons and the Hambledon Maids in red ribbons. The sports reporter said that the girls "bowled, batted, ran and catches as well as most men could do".

"Catches" isn't wrong – writers could spell words however they wanted until the 1800s!

Tennis

Tennis had been played in some form since the 1100s, but by the 1700s it was played across England. In London, in 1768, the top tennis player in England was Mr Tomkins. Everyone was shocked when he was beaten 2–1 by a French woman, Madame Bunel.

Even worse for Mr Tomkins was that Madame Bunel was much older than him. She was 40 years old!

Madame Bunel wore a short skirt and a loose jacket so she could run and hit. Mr Tomkins was a sore loser and demanded a rematch. She beat him again: 4–2.

Boxing

In the 1700s, women were famous for being strong boxers. Elizabeth Wilkinson, known as the “championess”, invented fair rules and kit for boxing: cloth jackets, short white petticoats, white shorts and stockings and shoes. There was NO male “champion”!

Elizabeth Wilkinson challenged Hannah Highfield to a boxing match in 1722. Each woman held a silver coin in her hand as they boxed. The first to drop the coin lost the fight.

Later, in the 1800s, women boxers were told that fighting in public was against the law and many of them were arrested. Eight women boxers fought with policemen and ran away, too fast to be caught.

These impressive women fighters were quite forgotten by the 1900s, when boxing became known as a sport only for men.

4 The Invention of Ladies: Women Divided

In the 1800s, new factories made Great Britain a rich country, but forced working women into low-paid, dangerous work.

1800-1930

1800

Poor women are working in factories. Rich women are persuaded to be idle.

1850s

Breakthrough! Rich women campaign for poor women AND women's rights.

1914

Women work in wartime industries, doing men's jobs while they are away fighting in the First World War.

At the same time, rich women were taught to be "ladylike", wear expensive bulky clothing and stay indoors. Ladies were said to be shy and weak and needed to rest. Sport – like making money, or having adventures – was not for women, but that all changed when the country needed more workers during the First World War.

1920s	1928	1930
Women's clothes become less restrictive and they win some freedoms ... but football is banned in 1921.	All women get the vote by 1928.	Whether the "new women" were free to work and play is a big argument.

Horse riding

Even when rich ladies were supposed to stay at home, they still went horse riding. But to make room for their long skirts they had to ride side-saddle – with both legs on the same side of the horse.

Alicia Meynell, a skilled horsewoman, challenged her brother-in-law, Captain Flint, to a race at York racecourse in 1804. She was in the lead when her horse, called Vingarillo, went **lame** and she had to stop. More than 100,000 spectators watched the race, some carrying signs that read "PETTICOATS FOREVER".

The following year, Alicia raced Francis Buckle, the top jockey in England, in front of a crowd of 30,000 people. They were **neck and neck** over the 6.5-kilometre course, but at the last stage, Alicia Meynell took the lead and won.

From 1910, ladies started riding astride the horses. They wore knee-length coats to hide their bottoms.

The Olympics

The Olympic Games began as a celebration of sport by the Ancient Greeks, probably as early as 776 BCE. Inspired by the Ancient Greeks, the modern Olympics began in 1896, and women competed for the first time in 1900.

Tennis

In the 1800s, tennis was very popular with rich women who had gardens big enough for a grass court. The Wimbledon Club in London held a singles match for "Ladies", where Maud Watson beat her sister Lilian. Maud won 54 matches, one after the other, until 1886 when she was defeated by Charlotte Dod.

In 1900, Charlotte Cooper, from Ealing in London, was the first woman Olympic tennis champion.

Charlotte Cooper

She became deaf at the age of 26, and won eight singles finals, one after the other – a record. She was Wimbledon's oldest ladies' champion at 37. Not only was she the first woman to triumph at the Olympics, she was also the first with a disability – 60 years before the Paralympic Games began.

Charlotte "Lottie" Dod

Lottie was only nine years old when she started playing tennis with her family in 1880, and at 15 she won her first Wimbledon title – the youngest ever singles tennis champion.

Lottie went on to win four more Wimbledon championships.
AND she was the British National Golf champion in 1904, AND she played in the national hockey squad, AND won a silver medal for archery in the 1908 Olympics.
She was one of the greatest athletes ever.

Golf

Everyone agreed that golf was suitable for ladies, because it was gentle walking in fresh air, but doctors advised that women should not hit the ball too hard or walk too far! Women golfers were not going to be stopped by bad advice, though.

By the end of the 1800s, there were more than 60 ladies' clubs in England and Scotland. It was a woman – Issette Pearson – who invented the system to score golfers. It was such a good system that a version of it is still used today.

Lady Margaret Scott won the first three British Ladies **Amateur** competitions from 1893. But her father, Lord Eldon, gave her acceptance speech.

Margaret Scott

Margaret Scott won two more championships, but stopped playing when she married in 1897.

Women golfers were banned from many golf courses and they had to stand aside if a man was playing behind them.

Cycling

For many women in the early 1900s, the new two-wheel bicycle was their gateway to freedom. At last, they could travel long distances without a man paying their bus fare.

But doctors warned that women could strain their hearts or twist their spines while cycling. One American doctor warned women that they would develop "bicycle-face", with their eyes and ears moving towards the nose.

Sixteen-year-old Tessie Reynolds set a record for cycling from Brighton to London and back again – roughly 193 kilometres – in just eight hours 38 minutes in 1893.

But the official racing organisation refused to recognise a record set by a woman.

Tessie Reynolds

Hockey

Hockey was first played in England in 1861, but ladies were separated from working women. The All-England Women's Hockey **Association** (1895) was for ladies only. These rich women could play in the daytime when most women had to work, and the association charged high fees that poorer women could not afford. The association said hockey was "too violent an exercise and ... strain for those who often spend much of their time in heavy manual work."

Working women set up their own Ladies' Hockey League in 1910, which was popular among the many women workers of the industrial towns in the north.

Cricket

The 1870s saw cricket rise in popularity as some schools allowed girls to play. But adult cricket clubs were for men only!
Everything changed in 1926, when a group of women hockey players founded the Women's Cricket Association.

Hockey player Marjorie Pollard was the first woman to **commentate** on sport for the BBC.

Football

Women led football into the 1800s. In 1881, 2,000 spectators paid to see the Scottish women's football team play the England women's team at Easter Road, Edinburgh. Scotland won 3–0. At a rematch in Glasgow, hundreds of spectators ran onto the pitch and the players had to escape!

In 1894, a young woman calling herself by a great false name, "Nettie Honeyball", advertised for players to join a women's football club. Lady Florence Dixie, an explorer and war reporter, helped Nettie to start the British Ladies Football Club. Lady Florence chose the kit: bloomers (big shorts, like those worn by women cyclists), **shinpads** and proper boots, so that they could play without their clothes getting in the way.

Nettie Honeyball, back row, second from the left, with the British Ladies FC North team in 1895

Lady Florence Caroline Dixie

Lady Florence was born in Dumfries, Scotland, in 1855. She loved playing sport, cut her hair short and refused to wear dresses. Like her brothers, she enjoyed swimming, riding and hunting and, although she hated school, she loved poetry and writing. In 1878, she went to Patagonia in South America and wrote the book *Across Patagonia*, which became a bestseller. In 1881, she became the first woman **war correspondent**, reporting from South Africa for the *Morning Post*. Lady Florence spent her life writing about women's rights and campaigning for equality.

Dick, Kerr Ladies Football Club in 1921

During the First World War (1914–1918), women workers in wartime factories often played football in their lunch breaks. One factory, called Dick, Kerr, set up a team. The Dick, Kerr Ladies team was more popular than any men's team, even when men returned to football after the war. Their Boxing Day match in 1920 at Goodison Park sold out to 53,000 fans.

After the war, women were persuaded to give up work so that men could return to their jobs, and it seemed as if nobody wanted sporty independent women. The English Football Association ruled that football was "not fitted for females" and banned women's teams. Men doctors said football was a "most unsuitable game, too much for a woman's physical frame". From the 1920s, football became a men's game.

Archery

The most famous woman archer was Alice Legh, who won the British National Championship 23 times between 1881 and 1922. Legh also won the World Championship in 1908.

Alice and her fellow archers complained that their clothes, a whale-boned corset and hooped skirt, stopped them from competing freely. By 1903, Alice added loose sleeves made from a light material that allowed her to draw her bow. And by the 1908 Olympics, competitors were wearing skirts and loose blouses.

Swimming

Professional swimming was popular among women – but they could not swim in public swimming pools with men.

Belle White, the first British diver to win an Olympic medal in 1912, was only allowed to practise diving from the high board at Highgate Men's Ponds once a week – when men were absent.

Belle White

In 1924, Lucy Morton won Olympic gold in the 200-metres breaststroke. Blackpool Council opened the local pool just for her, before and after her day's work at the Post Office.

Lucy Morton

Gymnastics

In the 1800s, poor children were so unfit that schools started "physical education" (PE) lessons. Girls did gymnastics and boys marched and ran.

But girl gymnasts were not allowed to enter any competitions until 1904. Another 24 years later, women were welcomed to the 1928 Olympics in Amsterdam, where the Great Britain team won a bronze medal.

Athletics

In 1923, the Women's Amateur Athletic Association held its first championship, and Mary Lines stood out. She went on to win nine gold, two silver and one bronze medal at international competitions.

Mary Lines

By 1928, the Olympic committee had finally introduced five women's events. But progress didn't last long! Even though women runners successfully completed the new 800-metre race, reports said they had "collapsed" at the end. The committee believed the false reports, and women were banned from the 800-metre race until 1960.

Dorothy Odam-Tyler won Silver in the high jump at Berlin in 1936.

5 Women Enter the World

In the Second World War, women had to join the Army, Navy or Air Force or do war work. When peace came, women were expected to stop working and go back home. But this time it wasn't so easy to push women back. During the mid-1900s there were huge protests.

1930 onwards

Second World War. Women are employed as equals to men while the country is at war.

1939–1945

Women are persuaded back into home life.

1945–1960

Women begin demanding equal pay and opportunities.

1960s

Grandmothers, mothers, aunts and their friends campaigned for better opportunities for women.

But there were no equal chances in sport. Only about a third of women and girls played sports – less than in many other countries.

But that third of women inspired the next generation!

The 1975 Sex Discrimination Act makes it easier for women to participate in sport.

The London Olympics have more women athletes than any other summer games.

Tokyo Olympics – women compete in all 33 sports.

1975

2012

2021

Figure Skating

Cecilia Colledge

At age 11, ice skater Cecilia Colledge was the youngest ever British Olympian, finishing eighth at the 1932 Winter Games. Four years later she won silver. She was the first woman skater to perform a double jump, and she invented two new skating moves: the camel spin and the layback spin. During the Second World War, Cecilia stopped skating to serve as an ambulance driver. But she lost none of her skills and went on to win the national title for the sixth time in 1946.

Cycling

In 1939, Marguerite Wilson became Britain's first full-time professional female cyclist. She broke the world record for cycling from one end of the UK to the other – 1,600 kilometres – in just under three days. By 1941, she held every women's cycling award.

In 1967, cyclist Beryl Burton set a 12-hour time trial record, faster than any man.

Women's cycling was not recognised as an Olympic sport until 1984 – that's 88 years after the men's!

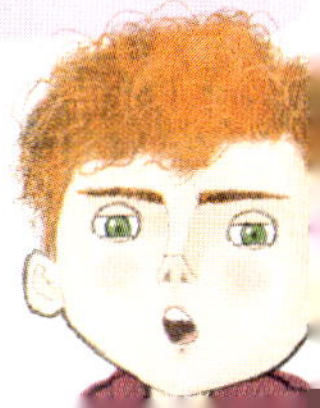

Athletics

Maureen Gardner was a ballerina who took up running to improve her health and clearly found a new skill – at the 1948 Olympics, she won a silver medal in the 80-metre hurdles!

Athletes like Linda Ludgrove, Mary Rand and Mary Peters were told by doctors (for no good reason) that they couldn't train hard. They ignored this advice and began lifting weights with strict training schedules.

In 1964, the women's athletics team won a record-breaking five medals out of 12 events. In comparison, the men only took seven medals from their 24 events!

One of the winners in 1964, Mary Rand, won a gold medal and broke the world record in the long jump. She also took silver in the pentathlon and bronze in the 4 × 100 metre relay.

Maureen Gardner

Tessa Sanderson competed at every Olympics from 1976 to 1996, and won gold in the javelin in 1984, becoming the first Black British woman to win a gold medal.

Tessa Sanderson

In the 1990s, Sally Gunnell became the only British female athlete to have won Olympic, World, European and **Commonwealth** titles in the same event – hurdling – and the only woman to have done this over 400 metres.

Sally Gunnell

In 2002, long-distance runner Paula Radcliffe broke the world marathon record by one and half minutes. Kelly Holmes shot to fame in 2004 when she won gold in the 800-metre and the 1500-metre races at the Athens Olympics – the only British athlete to win over both distances.

Paralympics

The first international Paralympic Games took place in 1960 in Rome, Italy. Margaret Maughan became Britain's first gold medallist at these games, winning in both archery and swimming.

Tanni Grey-Thompson

Tanni Grey-Thompson's sporting career started when she was just 13 years old. She rose to fame in 1988 with a bronze medal in Seoul for wheelchair racing and went on to win 11 more gold and four silver medals.

Cricket

Cricket continued to be popular with women through the 20th century. In 1971, pioneering sportswoman Rachael Heyhoe Flint set up the first cricket Women's World Cup and captained the England international squad. She also persuaded Marylebone Cricket Club to give women permission to play at their men-only ground.

Horse riding

Horse riding is still the only Olympic sport in which men and women compete against each other. Women were first allowed into **dressage** at the 1952 Olympics, and showjumping in 1956, when Britain's Pat Smythe and her horse Flanagan won bronze.

dressage

showjumping

eventing

Rugby

The first official women's rugby team, the Edinburgh University Amazons, was formed in 1962. Deborah Griffin and Carol Isherwood established the Women's Rugby Football Union in 1983 – a year before the men's leagues were formed! The first women's Rugby World Cup took place in 1991 in Wales, with the USA winning. By 2014, England had professional women rugby players and there are now over 500 clubs.

Boxing

An exhibition match for women's boxing in 1904 could not return the sport to women. It took nearly 100 years before a British woman could get a licence to box, and Jane Couch won her match in 1998. In 2012, women boxed at the Olympics for the first time. Officials wanted women fighters to wear skirts until a **petition** by Londoner Elizabeth Plank forced them to agree that they could wear shorts.

Nicola Adams

Nicola was born in Leeds in 1982. She went to her local boxing gym with her mum to keep fit and decided, at 13, that she was going to win an Olympic medal. But she had to find a coach and a boxing partner, as well as working as a builder and actor. Nicola Adams made history at London 2012 as the first woman ever to win an Olympic gold medal for boxing. In 2016, with the nation cheering her on, she did it again!

Football

The Women's Football Association carried on calling for women to be allowed to play, and, in 1971, the first Women's FA Cup Final went ahead, followed by the first England women's international match in 1972. It took them 50 years to get back on the pitch!

Women have continued to make football news. In 2022, the England women's team defeated Germany in the Euros. They won 2–1 in extra time at Wembley – the first international win for any England team since 1966. At the time of writing, the English women's football team is one of the world leaders and the "Lionesses", as they're called, attract crowds as big as the "Lions" – the men's team.

Making a difference

This is a great place to end this book about sportswomen – with fantastic successes – because what women can do depends on what women believe about themselves ...

When people tell girls and women they are weak, encourage them to stay at home, concentrate on how they look and not on what they can do – then women step back. But girls and women who want to play sport and believe in themselves do well.

As this history shows, even successful sportswomen can be pushed out – like the boxers and runners of the 1700s and the footballers of the 1900s. If we want successful sportswomen, and if we want women to enjoy sport, we have to make sure that everyone can play: boys and girls, men and women.

Glossary

amateur	a performer or sportsperson who isn't paid
association	a group of people who join together to achieve a goal
Civil War	war fought between groups of people who live in the same country
commentate	to report on an event for TV or radio
Commonwealth	an international association of countries, including the UK
convent	an all-women religious house
dressage	a competition in which a rider asks their horse to perform a series of controlled movements
fire walkers	performers who walked barefoot over hot stones
jousting	a sport of fighting on horseback using a lance
lame	unable to walk well because of damage to a leg
lance	a long spear
neck and neck	level with each other
parliament	a group of people who run a country

petticoats	undergarments worn under a skirt
petition	a written request for change
shinpads	thick material worn inside each sock to protect the lower part of the legs
war correspondent	a journalist who reports from a war

Index

A timeline of women in sport

1066–1500s

Women could be acrobats, firewalkers and hunters.

1500s

Women were increasingly recognised as fast runners and strong fighters.

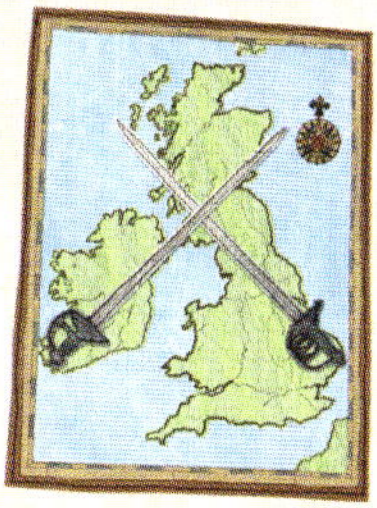

1600s

Sport was banned after the English Civil War until 1660.

1726

The first ever football match, played by women, took place.

1900

Women competed at the Olympics for the first time.

Women's clothes became less restrictive and they won some freedoms ... but football was banned in 1921.

In 2022, the Lionesses won England's first international football tournament since 1966.

1920s

2020–today

1908

Lottie Dod became one of the greatest female athletes in tennis, golf, hockey and archery!

2012

Jessica Ennis became the first British athlete to win gold in the heptathlon at the London 2012 Olympic Games.

Ideas for reading

Written by Stephanie Austwick
Primary Literacy Consultant

Reading objectives:

- retrieve, record and present information from non-fiction
- draw inferences and justify inferences with evidence
- summarise the main ideas drawn from more than one paragraph, identifying key details that support the main ideas

Spoken language objectives:

- listen and respond appropriately to adults and their peers
- participate in discussions, presentations, performances, role play, improvisations and debates
- consider and evaluate different viewpoints, attending to and building on the contributions of others

Curriculum links: PSHE: physical health and mental wellbeing; History: changes in an aspect of social history

Interest words: participate, opportunities, inspired

Resources: individual whiteboards or paper

Build a context for reading

- Look at the front cover and read the blurb together. Discuss what the term '*normal women in sport*' might mean. Explain that this is a historical non-fiction book that looks at the history of women in sport, as sport is for everyone. Some successful sportswomen become famous. Do children know any?
- Ask children if they know anything about women playing sport in the 'olden days'. Did their grandmothers play sports? Are there any sports they are particularly interested in finding out about?

Understand and apply reading strategies

- Open the book at the contents page and invite children to skim-read the chapter titles. Ask them what they notice about the organisation of the chapters – that they are chronological. Discuss the fact that, although this is an information text, the story still unfolds over time: we read historical information chapters chronologically so that we can understand how events and attitudes have developed over time.